LIFE S(

Leading Lady in Your Life Story

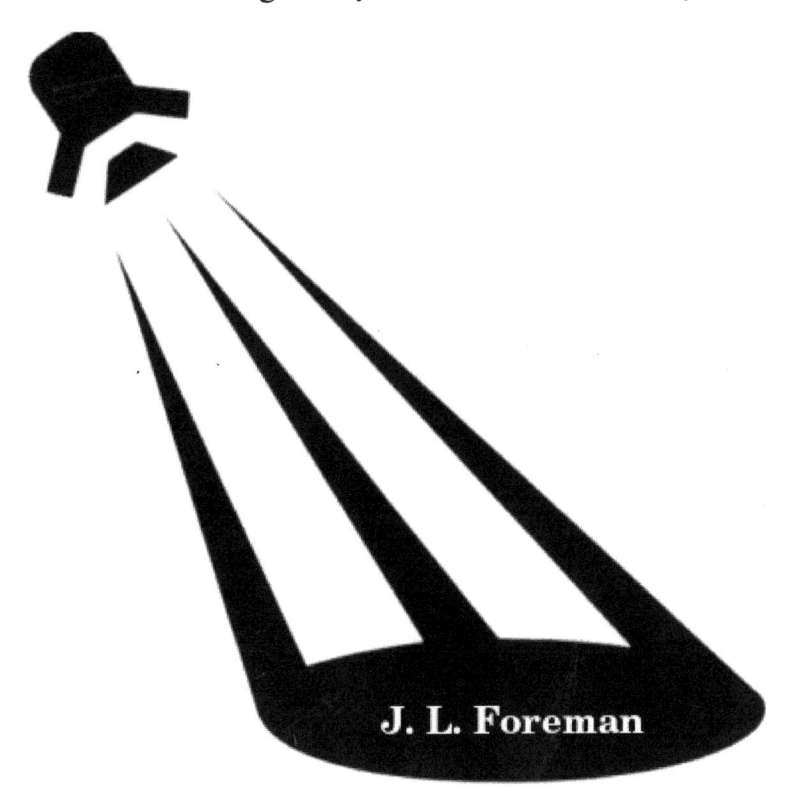

J. L. Foreman

Table of Contents

Setting the Stage 1

Unveiling the Script – Aligning with God's Purpose for You 3

The Audition – Preparing for Life's Challenges 11

The Callback – After the Audition 17

Casting Yourself as the Star – Taking Control of Your Life 25

Assembling the Cast – Building Your Support System 31

Directing the Supporting Cast – Managing Relationships 39

Rehearsing for Success – Practice Makes Perfect 47

Showtime – Stepping into the Spotlight 57

Behind the Scenes – Building Inner Strength 67

Handling Criticism – Navigating the Reviews 75

Encore! Maintaining Your Star Status 85

The Curtain Call – Stepping Fully into Your Role 93

This book is dedicated to the first Leading Lady in my life—my mother, the late *Evangelist Bernice Reid Foreman*. Your strength, faith, and love continue to inspire me every day.

To my only sister, *Vernest*, who has shown me how to stand tall and lead, even in the hardest times—I am forever grateful for your example.

And to the Leading Ladies who follow—my beautiful daughters *Joitwanae, D'Aria, and Angel*—I love you deeply. You are my heart, and I pray that you embrace your role as the stars of your own stories.

"Keep Shining"

Life Script: Leading Lady in Your Life Story

Copyright © 2024 by J. L. Foreman

All rights reserved. No part of this publication may be reproduced, distributed, or transmitted in any form or by any means, including photocopying, recording, or other electronic or mechanical methods, without the prior written permission of the publisher, except in the case of brief quotations embodied in critical reviews and certain other noncommercial uses permitted by copyright law.

Scripture References: Unless otherwise indicated, all Scripture quotations are taken from the New Revised Standard Version Bible (NRSV), copyright © 1989 by the Division of Christian Education of the National Council of the Churches of Christ in the United States of America. Used by permission. All rights reserved.

NKJV: Scripture quotations marked (NKJV) are taken from the New King James Version®. Copyright © 1982 by Thomas Nelson. Used by permission. All rights reserved.

NIV: Scripture quotations marked (NIV) are taken from the Holy Bible, New International Version®, NIV®. Copyright © 1973, 1978, 1984, 2011 by Biblica, Inc. Used by permission. All rights reserved worldwide.

ESV: Scripture quotations marked (ESV) are taken from The Holy Bible, English Standard Version®. Copyright © 2001 by Crossway Bibles, a publishing ministry of Good News Publishers. Used by permission. All rights reserved.

Cover Design: J. L. Foreman

Setting the Stage

Welcome to your Life Script. You may not have realized it, but you've been part of a grand production from the very beginning. God, the ultimate Playwright, wrote the script for your life with great care and purpose. Each moment, each decision, and each chapter has been leading you to this point. Now, it's time to step into the spotlight and embrace the role you were created for.

The idea of life as a stage is not new. Shakespeare famously said, "All the world's a stage, and all the men and women merely players." But long before Shakespeare penned those words, God had already written the greatest script of all—your life.

In this book, you will learn to see your life through a new lens. No longer will you be the understudy, standing on the sidelines, waiting for your moment to shine. Instead, you'll understand that you are the Leading Lady in your own story, uniquely designed for the role you're meant to play.

Every woman likes a "happy ending" or a good love story. We are happy when we hear of our friends or family getting that promotion or starting that business they have always talked about. We are happy when our girlfriends say they have found love. But deep inside, we sometimes feel envious. We desire a better position, a different career, dream that our own business ideas would finally get off the ground or wish for that special person to come into our own lives. We wonder and ask, "Where is the 'happy ending' in my Life Story?"

Over time, we may find that we no longer hold the role of the Leading Lady in our own life. Instead, we've been cast as an understudy or secondary character. When we take a close look at our lives, we may see that each stage feels mediocre or far from what we once imagined. In the pursuit of the things, we think will change our lives for the better, we sometimes realize that we don't even love the life we are living. This pursuit leads us back to ourselves, allowing us to reflect on why we're searching so hard for something else—something that sometimes makes us feel desperate.

Eventually, we are led to a place of reflection and meditation, where the words of Proverbs 3:6 come to mind: "In all your ways acknowledge him, and he will make straight your paths." We discover that the reason we cannot attain the role of the Leading Lady is that we have not fully "walked the WALK."

If you have allowed others—narrators and critics—to direct your path, your success in becoming the Leading Lady has been limited. You may have missed important instructions from the "Director" and not valued the support of the "Crew." It's now time for you to understand your Role and step onto the path of loving yourself and learning to be happy with where you are and what you've accomplished.

As Maya Angelou once said, "Success is liking yourself, liking what you do, and liking how you do it." If you don't feel successful and the reviews of your life story don't show you as the Star, it's time to rewrite the script.

Unveiling the Script – Aligning with God's Purpose for You

You've spent years watching others take center stage, haven't you? Their successes, their triumphs, their "happy endings"—all unfolding right before your eyes while you stood in the wings, waiting for your moment. But here's the truth, dear sister: you were never meant to be an understudy in your own life story. God has written you as the star, and it's time you embraced that role with all your heart.

To rewrite your life story and cast yourself as the "Star"—the "Leading Lady"—you must start at the very beginning. You need to see yourself and your character the way the Playwright envisioned you. You were uniquely designed for this role.

Created for a Purpose

From the start, God saw the need for a companion for Adam, uniquely designed to complement and complete him. **Genesis 2:20b-23** recounts, *"But for the man there was not found a helper as his partner. So the Lord God caused a deep sleep to fall upon the man, and he slept; then He took one of his ribs and closed up its place with flesh. And the rib that the Lord God had taken from the man He made into a woman and brought her to the man. Then the man said, 'This at last is bone of my bones and flesh of my flesh; this one shall be called Woman, for out of Man this one was taken.'"*

You were cunningly fashioned with great intention. God didn't just create you to fill space—He designed you with a divine purpose that only you can fulfill. **Psalm 139:13-14** reminds us, *"For it was You who formed my inward parts; You knit me together in my mother's womb. I praise You, for I am fearfully and wonderfully made."* God made no mistakes when He created you; you are His masterpiece.

A Royal Role

Not only were you designed with purpose, but you were also chosen. You are part of God's royal family. **1 Peter 2:9** declares, *"But you are a chosen race, a royal priesthood, a holy nation, God's own people, in order that you may proclaim the mighty acts of Him who called you out of darkness into His marvelous light."* You were created for this role, and you have everything you need to shine in it.

The Role of a Leading Lady

The Playwright envisioned a woman who is not just beautiful and capable but adaptable and complementary. You, as the Leading Lady, have been made to fit this role perfectly. But sometimes, stepping into that role can feel overwhelming. Have you ever doubted yourself? Wondered if you're really the one for the job?

God knows you might feel uncertain at times. Yet, it's not about how the world sees you or even how you see yourself. It's about who you are in God. **Romans 8:37** tells us, *"No, in all these things we are more than conquerors through Him who loved us."* Sister, you are more than enough because God has already declared you victorious.

Embracing Your Role

Affirm Your Worth: Start by affirming your identity as God's chosen. Begin each day by declaring aloud who you are in Christ.

- **Scripture***: "For we are what He has made us, created in Christ Jesus for good works, which God prepared beforehand to beforehand to be our way of life." –* **Ephesians 2:10**
- **Application:** Create a list of affirmations rooted in Scripture about your worth and purpose. Say them out loud every morning, affirming the truth of God's promises over your life.

See Yourself Through God's Eyes: How often do you focus on your flaws or limitations? Start seeing yourself the way God sees you—strong, capable, and uniquely prepared for every challenge.

- **Scripture**: *"I praise You, for I am fearfully and wonderfully made. Wonderful are Your works; that I know very well."* **Psalm 139:14**
- **Application**: Write down moments when you feel insecure or doubtful. Then, reflect on **Psalm 139:14** to remind yourself that you are beautifully crafted by God.

Preparation for Your Role

Just like any Leading Lady, preparation is key. An actress rehearses, studies her role, and works on perfecting her craft. You, too, must commit to growth and reflection. God doesn't expect you to be perfect overnight. He simply asks for your willingness to grow and be molded by Him.

Proverbs 31:10 says, *"A capable wife who can find? She is far more precious than jewels."* This verse isn't just about being a wife; it's about the incredible value King Lemuel found in the woman he loved. To him, she was more precious than any treasure, her worth far exceeding that of the finest jewels. It's a powerful reminder that your value isn't tied to a title or role—it's about the character, strength, and grace that you embody.

God crafted you with intention and care. You are fearfully and wonderfully made, uniquely precious in His eyes, fully capable of fulfilling the special role He has for you. So, the next time you question your value, think of how God sees you—priceless, just like that woman King Lemuel treasured.

You must also embrace that growth is a process. **Psalm 37:23-24** reassures us, *"Our steps are made firm by the Lord, when He delights in our way; though we stumble, we shall not fall headlong, for the Lord holds us by the hand."* Even when you falter, God holds you up, directing your steps.

Preparing for Your Role

Commit to Spiritual Growth: Set aside intentional time each day to pray, study Scripture, and reflect on God's Word.

- **Scripture:** *"Your word is a lamp to my feet and a light to*

my path." – **Psalm 119:105**
- **Application:** Start each day with prayer and Scripture reading. Choose one verse to meditate on throughout the day, asking God to guide your steps.

Self-Reflect: Growth starts with self-reflection. What are the areas God is calling you to work on? What habits or thoughts is He asking you to let go of?

- **Scripture:** *"Examine yourselves to see whether you are living in the faith."* – **2 Corinthians 13:5**
- **Application:** Spend time each week reflecting on where you've grown and where you need to grow. Journal your thoughts, asking God to help strengthen your areas of weakness.

Stepping into the Role with Confidence

It's time to walk boldly into your role. You are not a supporting character in someone else's story—you are the Leading Lady. God created you to shine, to inspire, and to lead. How you see yourself matters. If you believe you're unworthy or unprepared, that will show. But if you embrace the confidence God has given you, you'll step into the role He's written with grace and assurance.

James 1:2-4 encourages us: *"My brothers and sisters, whenever you face trials of any kind, consider it nothing but joy, because you know that the testing of your faith produces endurance; and let endurance have its full effect, so that you may be mature and complete, lacking in nothing."*

God doesn't call those who are already fully qualified—He qualifies those He calls. Every trial, setback, and lesson is a tool He uses to prepare you for the next step.

Stepping into Your Role

Walk in Confidence: Face each day knowing that God has equipped you for every challenge. See yourself the way He sees you.

- **Scripture**: *"For God gave us a spirit not of fear but of power and love and self-discipline."* – **2 Timothy 1:7**
- **Application**: When fear or insecurity creeps in, remember **2 Timothy 1:7**. Say it out loud and use it to replace the doubts with God's truth.

Embrace Your Trials: Your struggles aren't roadblocks—they're steppingstones to your purpose. Use them to grow and prepare for your destiny.

- **Scripture**: *"Count it all joy, my brothers and sisters, when you meet trials of various kinds."* – **James 1:2**
- **Application**: Reflect on past trials that have shaped you. Write down what you've learned from each experience and how God has used it to prepare you for your future.

Get Ready for the Role of a Lifetime

Now that you've seen the role God created for you, it's time to fully embrace it. Don't shy away from the spotlight He's placed on you—this is your moment. Step forward, knowing that God has instilled in you everything you need for this role.

Your identity is not in a title, but in who God says you are. Step confidently into your destiny, knowing that you were chosen for such a time as this. You are the Leading Lady of your life's story, and your purpose is far greater than you could ever imagine.

Scripture References:

- Genesis 2:20b-23
- Psalm 139:13-14
- 1 Peter 2:9
- Romans 8:37
- Ephesians 2:10
- Proverbs 31:10
- Psalm 37:23-24
- Psalm 119:105
- 2 Corinthians 13:5
- 2 Timothy 1:7
- James 1:2-4

The Audition – Preparing for Life's Challenges

Ladies, Ladies, Ladies! Calling all women who know they've got what it takes to be the Leading Lady. You've been preparing, working hard to change the things that keep you as the understudy, even though you auditioned for the lead. Deep down, you already have the qualities that set you apart in your own life story. Reflect on your journey and see yourself the way the Playwright—God—sees you. You dress the part, walk the walk, and talk the talk. And now, here you are, auditioning.

The audition notice reads:

- I'm looking for that woman who will be a dreamer.
- That woman who will be a leader.
- That woman who will be a teacher.
- That woman who will be an entrepreneur.
- That woman who will be a servant.
- That woman who will be a minister.
- That woman who will be a wife.
- That woman who will be a mother.

Are you the one?

Sometimes, we try to promote ourselves, chasing after the roles we think fit us best. We attempt to mold the character to our comfort zone rather than allowing God to shape us into the character He has called us to be. Sure, our self-promotion might land us some roles, but they don't always make us the star. Often, we end up in supporting roles—and there's nothing wrong with that. But does it align with your life's story?

To be the Leading Lady in your life, you need support, especially when you struggle to encourage yourself. Finding the right "auditions" and positioning yourself where you truly belong requires guidance. Think of it this way: just like an actress needs an agent to help navigate the industry, you need an Agent who can connect you with your purpose. Agents might take a cut of what you get, but they guide you toward the lead role that's meant for you. The Playwright of your life knew you'd need a special Agent to keep you on track. That Agent is connected to the perfect Director.

Who Is Your Agent?

Who's guiding you? Have you found the Agent who promotes you and acts on your behalf? **Romans 8:26** says, *"Likewise the Spirit helps us in our weakness; for we do not know how to pray as we ought, but that very Spirit intercedes with sighs too deep for words."* The Holy Spirit is your Agent, advocating for you and working behind the scenes, especially when you don't even know how to express what you need.

And who is your Director? **John 14:16** tells us, *"And I will ask the Father, and he will give you another Advocate, to be with you forever."* Jesus Christ is the Director, guiding your steps and making sure you stay on the path toward becoming the Leading Lady in your life.

From Audition to Stardom: Key Principles to Live By

From the moment you audition for life's challenges to the day you achieve your dreams, keep these key principles in mind:

Be Positive:

- **Scripture:** *"I can do all things through him who strengthens me."* – **Philippians 4:13**
- **Application:** When challenges arise, shift your focus toward Christ's strength. When negative thoughts creep in, recite **Philippians 4:13** as an affirmation. Remember, with Christ, you have the power to overcome anything.

Be Confident:

- **Scripture:** *"I am confident of this, that the one who began a good work among you will bring it to completion by the day of Jesus Christ."* – **Philippians 1:6**
- **Application:** Take time to reflect on moments where you've seen God's hand in your life. Journal about past victories and spiritual growth, reminding yourself that God is still working in you. This reflection will boost your confidence as you move forward.

Maintain a Pleasant Attitude:

- **Scripture:** *"Finally, all of you, have unity of spirit, sympathy, love for one another, a tender heart, and a humble mind." –* **1 Peter 3:8**
- **Application:** Show kindness and empathy in your daily interactions. When conflicts arise, pause, breathe, and approach the situation with a spirit of love and humility. You'll see that keeping a positive attitude changes not only your outlook but also how others respond to you.

Listen to Directions:

- **Scripture:** *"Listen, children, to a father's instruction, and be attentive, that you may gain insight; for I give you good precepts: do not forsake my teaching." –* **Proverbs 4:1-2**
- **Application:** Set aside quiet time to listen for God's guidance. After praying, pause to reflect on what God might be speaking to your heart. Write down any insights in a journal and actively apply them.

Follow Instructions:

- **Scripture:** *"Therefore be imitators of God, as beloved children." –* **Ephesians 5:1**
- **Application:** When you receive instructions from God through prayer or Scripture, take action. Create a list of steps to follow and review them regularly to make sure you're walking in obedience to His will.

Memorize Your Lines:

- **Scripture**: *"I treasure your word in my heart, so that I may*

not sin against you." – **Psalm 119:11**
- **Application:** Choose a Bible verse each week to memorize. Keep it close during moments of doubt, allowing it to remind you of God's promises.

Be Cooperative:

- **Scripture:** *"Making every effort to maintain the unity of the Spirit in the bond of peace."* – **Ephesians 4:3**
- **Application:** When working with others, strive for peace and unity by practicing active listening. Resolve conflicts with grace, always prioritizing harmony in your relationships.

Put on a Smile:

- **Scripture:** *"A glad heart makes a cheerful countenance..."* – **Proverbs 15:13a**
- **Application:** Start each day by practicing gratitude. Write down three things you're thankful for, and let that joy shine through in your demeanor. Your smile can encourage not only you but also those around you.

Preparing for Life's Challenges

Auditions can be intimidating, but with the Holy Spirit as your Agent and Jesus as your Director, you never face them alone. Life's auditions aren't about how perfectly you perform; they're about how much you trust the plan God has for you.

As you prepare for each challenge, remember the importance of spiritual preparation—prayer, studying God's Word, and trusting in His guidance. With every audition, you grow, learn, and step closer to that lead role that's been waiting for you all along. God is cheering you on from behind the scenes, making sure you're ready for when the curtains rise and you take your place as the Leading Lady.

Scripture References:

- Romans 8:26
- John 14:16
- Philippians 4:13
- Philippians 1:6
- 1 Peter 3:8
- Proverbs 4:1-2
- Ephesians 5:1
- Psalm 119:11
- Ephesians 4:3
- Proverbs 15:13a

The Callback – After the Audition

After every audition, there's that nerve-wracking period of waiting—right? It's the time between stepping out in faith and hearing if you've "made the cut." In life, these moments can be some of the most challenging. You've given it your all, but now, you find yourself standing in that tension between expectation and uncertainty. It's the waiting for the callback.

In the theater of life, the callback represents God's response to your faithfulness and obedience. Sometimes, this callback comes in the form of a clear opportunity or breakthrough. Other times, it feels like all you hear is silence. In those quiet moments, you may begin to doubt yourself—or worse, doubt God. But here's the truth: God's timing is always perfect. **Proverbs 3:5-6** reminds us, *"Trust in the Lord with all your heart, and do not rely on your own insight. In all your ways acknowledge Him, and He will make straight your paths."*

The waiting after the audition isn't passive—it's a time for spiritual growth, trust, and preparation. God is at work behind the scenes, refining you for something greater. The callback isn't just about whether you've "made it"—it's about God preparing you for the next chapter in your life.

The Importance of the Callback

The callback is a test of faith and perseverance. It's not just about getting validation or receiving what you want—it's about building your spiritual endurance. Waiting reveals your true motives and deepens your relationship with God. When you trust Him in the waiting, He renews your strength and prepares your heart for what's ahead.

Isaiah 40:31 offers a powerful promise: *"But those who wait for the Lord shall renew their strength, they shall mount up with wings like eagles, they shall run and not be weary, they shall walk and not faint."* Much like how performers build endurance through rehearsals, you build spiritual resilience by trusting God during the waiting.

Waiting Isn't Wasted

God's timing is deliberate, and He often does His greatest work during the times we feel most uncertain. Just because you don't see movement doesn't mean God is inactive. Think of a seed growing beneath the soil—there's growth happening before it even breaks through to the light. **Psalm 27:14** encourages us, *"Wait for the Lord; be strong, and let your heart take courage; wait for the Lord!"*

Trusting God's Timing

Learning to trust God's timing can be one of the hardest parts of the waiting process. We want results right away—who doesn't crave the satisfaction of knowing how things will turn out? But God works on a timeline that's designed for both our growth and His glory. **Ecclesiastes 3:1** reminds us, *"For everything there is a season, and a time for every matter under heaven."* Even when the wait feels endless, trust that God's timing is part of His perfect plan for you.

What Does It Mean to Trust God's Timing?

Release Control: Waiting forces us to let go of control. We often think we know the best timing for our lives, but God's perspective is infinitely greater. Sometimes, the delay isn't because you're not ready—it's because the opportunity isn't ready for you yet. Learning to release control is a sign of spiritual maturity.

- **Scripture**: *"The human mind plans the way, but the Lord directs the steps."* – **Proverbs 16:9**
- **Application**: Take a moment to reflect on where you've been trying to control the outcome. Pray for the grace to release your need for control and trust in God's timing.

Active Waiting: Waiting on God doesn't mean sitting around doing nothing. It means continuing to prepare, to serve, and to trust. During this time, God is equipping you with the tools needed for the next step in your journey.

- **Scripture**: *"So let us not grow weary in doing what is right, for we will reap at harvest time, if we do not give up."* – **Galatians 6:9**
- **Application**: While you wait, focus on growing in your faith. Study the Word, strengthen your prayer life, and seek opportunities to serve others. When the callback comes, you'll be spiritually ready.

The Power of Patience

In today's fast-paced world, waiting is one of the hardest things to do. But the period after the audition is a sacred time where God teaches you patience. Patience isn't just the ability to wait—it's how you act while you're waiting. James 1:4 encourages us, "Let endurance have its full effect, so that you may be mature and complete, lacking in nothing." God uses patience to develop your character, refining you into the person He's called you to be.

How to Cultivate Patience

Focus on Growth: Instead of viewing waiting as wasted time, think of it as a period of spiritual growth. Use this time to deepen your relationship with God and reflect on the lessons He's teaching you.

- **Scripture**: *"My brothers and sisters, whenever you face trials of any kind, consider it nothing but joy, because you know that the testing of your faith produces endurance."* – **James 1:2-3**
- **Application**: Write down the ways you've grown in past seasons of waiting. Reflect on how God used those times to strengthen your faith and develop your character. Let that serve as a reminder of the growth happening now.

Find Purpose in the Waiting: Just as an actress uses downtime to refine her lines and character, use the waiting period to focus on what God is calling you to develop in yourself. There's always purpose in the waiting.

- **Scripture**: *"Wait for the Lord; be strong, and let your heart take courage; wait for the Lord!"* – **Psalm 27:14**
- **Application**: Instead of focusing on what you're waiting

for, shift your perspective to how God is preparing you for what's next. What areas of your life can you nurture or strengthen while you wait?

What Happens After the Callback?

The callback marks the beginning of a new phase, not the end of the journey. Once you receive confirmation that you're moving forward, there's work to be done. **Philippians 3:13b -14** encourages us, *"Forgetting what lies behind and straining forward to what lies ahead, I press on toward the goal for the prize of the heavenly call of God in Christ Jesus."* The callback is God's way of telling you that you're on the right track—but now you must step forward with renewed commitment.

How to Step Forward After the Callback

Let Go of the Past: Sometimes, moving forward requires letting go of past disappointments, mistakes, or even successes. Don't let past fears or failures hold you back from embracing the new opportunity that's before you.

- **Scripture**: *"So if anyone is in Christ, there is a new creation: everything old has passed away; see, everything has become new!"* – **2 Corinthians 5:17**
- **Application**: Reflect on any areas where you may be holding on to the past. Pray for the strength to release what's behind and embrace the new opportunities God is calling you into.

Act on the Opportunity: The callback is a signal that it's time to act. Like a performer who gets the role, you now need to step into your calling with purpose and intention.

- **Scripture: Ephesians 5:15-16a** tells us, *"Be careful then how you live, not as unwise people but as wise, making the most of the time..."*
- **Application**: Identify the next steps you need to take after the callback. Whether it's pursuing a new opportunity, deepening your faith, or stepping into a leadership role, take action and trust that God is guiding your steps.

The Joy of the Callback

The callback isn't just about progress—it's about confirmation. It's God's way of showing you that you're moving in the right direction and that He's with you every step of the way. **Jeremiah 29:11** reassures us, *"For surely I know the plans I have for you, says the Lord, plans for your welfare and not for harm, to give you a future with hope."* Celebrate the callback as a moment of God's faithfulness.

Even though the journey is far from over, the callback is a sign that God's promises are being fulfilled. Take joy in knowing that He's not done with you yet and that He is leading you toward the greater purpose He has designed for your life.

Scripture References:

- Proverbs 3:5-6
- Isaiah 40:31

- Ecclesiastes 3:1
- Proverbs 16:9
- Galatians 6:9
- James 1:2-3
- Psalm 27:14
- 2 Corinthians 5:17
- Philippians 3:13b-14
- Ephesians 5:15-16a
- Jeremiah 29:11

Casting Yourself as the Star – Taking Control of Your Life

The notices have gone out, and now it's time to assemble the cast for your life's production. This casting call has reached the world: *"For many are called, but few are chosen."* – **Matthew 22:14**. What many don't realize is that everyone in your life plays a role in your story.

Even Jesus, in His prayer, didn't ask the Father to remove His followers from the world but to protect them: *"I am not asking you to take them out of the world, but I ask you to protect them from the evil one. They do not belong to the world, just as I do not belong to the world. Sanctify them in the truth; your word is truth."* – **John 17:15-17**.

The people you surround yourself with will greatly impact your growth into the Leading Lady role God has for you. But you also need to know who truly has your best interests at heart and when it's time to distance yourself from influences that hold you back.

Choosing the Right Cast

Romans 12:2 reminds us: *"Do not be conformed to this world, but be transformed by the renewing of your mind, so that you may discern what is the will of God—what is good and acceptable and perfect."* Having the right inner circle is crucial to fulfilling your God-given role. Even in the Bible, leading figures had others who supported them on their journey:

- Elisha had Elijah.
- Moses had Aaron and Miriam.
- Esther had her uncle Mordecai.
- Ruth had Naomi.
- Jesus had His disciples—or rather, the disciples had Jesus.

Like those who surrounded these biblical figures, the people in your life play a key role in helping you step into the Leading Lady role. God looks at the heart, not outward appearances. Aligning yourself with His will is vital for fulfilling your role in His grand story. You can achieve success by the world's standards, but true fulfillment comes when you walk in alignment with God's purpose for your life.

God's Agent in Your Life

Your Heavenly Father won't leave you to figure things out on your own. **Luke 11:11-13** reveals God's heart for us: *"Is there anyone among you who, if your child asks for a fish, will give a snake instead? Or if the child asks for an egg, will give a scorpion? If you, who are evil, know how to give good gifts to your children, how much more will the Heavenly Father give the Holy Spirit to those who ask him!"*

God has given you the Holy Spirit—your personal Agent—who is always advocating for you and has your best interests at heart. The Holy Spirit guides you into the lead role that God has prepared. All you have to do is ask: *"Ask, and it will be given to you; seek, and you will find; knock, and the door will be opened to you."* – **Matthew 7:7**.

Taking Control of Your Life

Recognize Your Inner Circle: Evaluate the people in your life's cast. Are they helping you grow or holding you back? Surround yourself with those who push you toward your God-given purpose.

- **Scripture**: *"Do not be deceived: 'Bad company ruins good morals.'"* – **1 Corinthians 15:33**
- **Application**: Take a moment to assess your inner circle. Write down the names of those closest to you and reflect on whether they uplift and support your growth or lead you away from your purpose. Pray for wisdom in managing these relationships.

Rely on the Holy Spirit: Just as an actress trusts her agent to guide her career, trust the Holy Spirit to guide your life. The Holy Spirit is there to advocate for you, lead you, and equip you for your role.

- **Scripture**: *"When the Spirit of truth comes, he will guide you into all the truth."* – **John 16:13a**
- **Application**: Every day, ask the Holy Spirit for guidance. Before making any decision—big or small—pause and invite the Holy Spirit to direct your steps.

Separate Yourself When Necessary: Not everyone is meant to be part of your journey forever. Be willing to step back from relationships that no longer align with God's purpose for your life.

- **Scripture**: *"Do not be mismatched with unbelievers. For what partnership is there between righteousness and lawlessness? Or what fellowship is there between light and darkness?"* – **2 Corinthians 6:14**
- **Application**: If there is a relationship in your life that

drains your energy or leads you away from God's purpose, pray for wisdom on how to handle it. Be willing to distance yourself if needed to protect your spiritual growth.

Finding Success in God's Plan

You weren't designed to conform to the world's standards. While you may seek worldly success, the true fulfillment of your role as the Leading Lady comes when you align with God's vision for your life. Defining success on your own terms may bring temporary satisfaction, but in the long run, you'll miss the fullness of what God has in store for you.

Remember, God is generous and wants the best for you. **Luke 11:11-13** shows us that just as earthly parents want to give good gifts to their children, how much more does your Heavenly Father desire to equip you with everything you need for your journey? God has given you the Holy Spirit as your personal Agent, who will never fail you.

Trusting God's Plan for Success

Seek God's Vision for Your Life: Before pursuing any role or opportunity, ask God to reveal His vision for your life. Trust that His plan is far greater than anything you could imagine.

- **Scripture**: *"For I know the plans I have for you, says the Lord, plans for your welfare and not for harm, to give you a future with hope." –* **Jeremiah 29:11**
- **Application**: During your prayer time, ask God to show

you His vision for your life. Write down any insights or revelations and make decisions that align with that vision.

Embrace God's Timing: Success may not come in the timeline you expect, but God's timing is always perfect. Trust that He is working out every detail behind the scenes.

- **Scripture**: *"For everything there is a season, and a time for every matter under heaven."* – **Ecclesiastes 3:1**
- **Application**: When you feel anxious about the future, take a deep breath and remind yourself that God's timing is perfect. Surrender your timeline to Him, trusting that He will bring things to pass at the right moment.

What Are You Waiting For?

As the Leading Lady in your life, you've been given everything you need to succeed. You've been called and equipped. Now, all that's left for you to do is ask.

So, what are you waiting for? JUST ASK.

Scripture References:

- Matthew 22:14
- John 17:15-17
- Romans 12:2
- Luke 11:11-13
- Matthew 7:7
- John 16:13

- 1 Corinthians 15:33
- 2 Corinthians 6:14
- Jeremiah 29:11
- Ecclesiastes 3:1

Assembling the Cast – Building Your Support System

While God defines who we are, the people in our lives also play a crucial role in shaping us. They can bring out the best in us, but they can also bring out the worst. Unfortunately, people tend to remember the worst moments more than the best. To better understand this dynamic, let's look back to the beginning of time—to the creation of Adam and Eve—where their roles were clearly defined.

Genesis 1:1 tells us: *"In the beginning, God created the heavens and the earth."* Before placing us in our roles, God prepares the stage for our lives. In **Genesis 1:1**, that stage was the Garden of Eden. For us, the stage is our life's journey. After preparing the stage, God created man and woman and placed them into the story: *"And the Lord God planted a garden in Eden, in the east; and there He put the man whom He had formed."* – **Genesis 2:8**.

Before Eve was even created, God had already formed Adam and placed him on his stage—the Garden. But God saw that something was missing. Adam didn't have a helper, someone like him. So God, in His infinite creativity, took part of Adam—a rib—and skillfully formed Eve. The Hebrew word for "made" in **Genesis 2:22** is *"banah,"* which means "skillfully formed." Eve wasn't hastily thrown together; she was carefully crafted as a masterpiece by God Himself.

When Adam laid eyes on Eve, he immediately recognized her significance: *"This at last is bone of my bones and flesh of my flesh; she shall be called Woman, for out of Man this one was taken."* – **Genesis 2:23**.

Understanding Your Substance

Eve wasn't initially given a personal name—her identity was tied to her essence, her substance. As the Leading Lady of your life, you must also understand your substance—your talents, abilities, and gifts. Do you realize that you were *skillfully formed* by God for a specific purpose? **Ephesians 2:10** reminds us: *"For we are what He has made us, created in Christ Jesus for good works, which God prepared beforehand to be our way of life."* As you consider the roles people play in your life, it's essential to first know yourself.

Understanding the Cast in Your Life

As Eve's story unfolded, another cast member entered the scene—the serpent. When Adam named the serpent, it was just another creature in the garden, an extra cast member. But this serpent had its own ideas about the role it wanted to play. **Genesis 3:1** describes the serpent as *"more cunning than any other wild animal."* He wasn't intimidating by appearance, but his ability to influence made him dangerous.

Eve's interaction with the serpent changed her story. The serpent questioned her, challenging what God had commanded. Eve misquoted God's instructions, and the serpent used that moment to persuade her into eating the forbidden fruit. This sly adversary shifted the narrative of her life. After disobeying God, Eve and Adam's eyes were opened, and they saw themselves differently. They felt ashamed and tried to cover their nakedness by making undergarments and hiding from God.

When God called out to Adam, he responded, *"I heard you in the garden, and I was afraid because I was naked; so I hid."* Their relationship with God, with each other, and their roles had changed. When confronted, Adam blamed Eve, and Eve blamed the serpent. God cursed the serpent and declared the consequences of Adam and Eve's actions. Only after this did Adam name his wife Eve, for she was to become the mother of all living. Her identity now reflected her future role.

As the Leading Lady of your life, it's vital to know your name and calling—not defined by your mistakes, but by your essence. Eve may have stumbled, but her role in God's story remained significant.

Your Cast: Identifying Roles in Your Life

Just as God wrote the script for Eve's life, He has written the script for yours. Now, it's time to assess the cast members in your story. Who are they? What roles do they play?

- **God: The Playwright**
  God has written the script of your life and orchestrated

every detail. He knows the beginning, the middle, and the end.

- **You: The Leading Lady**
  You are the star of your story. You were created with purpose, skillfully formed to fulfill a role that no one else can play. You are the heroine of your life's story.

- **Your Supporting Cast**
  These are the people who add meaning and support to your journey. They are friends, mentors, family members, and colleagues who help you grow and fulfill your purpose. In the Bible, these people were like Aaron and Miriam to Moses, Mordecai to Esther, and Naomi to Ruth.

- **The Extras**
  Extras are people who come and go. They may not play a significant role, but they still impact your life in some way—coworkers, neighbors, or acquaintances. Their presence can influence you, even if their time in your life is brief.

- **The Adversary**
  The serpent in Eve's story represents the adversary—the one who opposes your progress and tries to pull you away from your role as the Leading Lady. The adversary can take many forms, from people who spread rumors about you to internal struggles like self-doubt or destructive habits. Stay vigilant. **1 Peter 5:8** warns us: *"Discipline yourselves, keep alert. Like a roaring lion your adversary the devil prowls around, looking for someone to devour."*

Assembling Your Support System

Identify Your Supporting Cast

Who are the people in your life that offer support and encouragement? Surround yourself with those who lift you up and help you grow.

- **Scripture**: *"Two are better than one, because they have a good reward for their toil."* – **Ecclesiastes 4:9**
- **Application**: List the key people who play a positive role in your life. Thank God for these individuals and look for ways to strengthen these relationships.

Recognize the Extras

Sometimes, the people we see as "extras" can have more impact than we realize. Be mindful of brief encounters and how they shape your daily experience.

- **Scripture**: *"Let each of you look not to your own interests, but to the interests of others."* – **Philippians 2:4**
- **Application**: Reflect on the people you might overlook in your daily life. How might they influence you, and how can you show them God's love, even in small ways?

Stay Aware of the Adversary

Be mindful of the forces that try to undermine your progress. Whether it's external influences or internal struggles, stay alert and guard your heart.

- **Scripture**: *"Put on the whole armor of God, so that you may be able to stand against the wiles of the devil."* – **Ephesians 6:11**
- **Application**: Consider areas in your life where the adversary might be interfering. Pray for discernment and strength to overcome these obstacles.

Maintaining Your Role as the Leading Lady

To maintain your role as the Leading Lady, you must continue seeking guidance from the ultimate Director—God. **Proverbs 3:5-6** reminds us to continue to trust in God with our whole heart and do not rely on our own understanding. But in everything you do seek God, and he will give you clear directions.

Take time to reflect on your current stage of life:

- Who is influencing your journey?
- How can you maintain your role as the Leading Lady?
- What steps will you take to prepare for the next act in your life's story?

Remember, this is the role of a lifetime, and God has already prepared you for it.

Scripture References:

- Genesis 1:1
- Genesis 2:8
- Genesis 2:22-23
- Ephesians 2:10

- Genesis 3:1
- 1 Peter 5:8
- Ecclesiastes 4:9
- Philippians 2:4
- Ephesians 6:11
- Proverbs 3:5-6

Directing the Supporting Cast – Managing Relationships

Understanding your Supporting Cast is crucial for success. The word *empower* means "to invest with power, especially legal or official authority," or "to equip or supply with ability; enable." When someone empowers you, you are then able to empower others.

Empowerment: A Powerful Investment

As the Leading Lady of your life story, this empowerment is critical. You now possess:

- **A power investment**: This is not superficial; it's real and substantial.
- **The equipment to enable**: You have the tools to help others reach their potential.
- **The ability to supplement someone else's abilities**: You can add to and uplift others, enhancing their capabilities.

Philippians 4:13 assures us: *"I can do all things through him who strengthens me."* You have been empowered through Christ, and now you have the ability to empower others.

Empowerment is like an investment. When you invest in the right people at the right time, the return is abundant. **Ecclesiastes 3:1-2** reminds us: *"For everything, there is a season, and a time for every matter under heaven: a time to be born, and a time to die; a time to plant, and a time to pluck up what is planted."* The key to a successful return is understanding where to seek help and how to utilize your network.

Networking: Building Your Circle

To achieve the best results in life, you need the right network. Just as a banker can't help you harvest a crop and a farmer can't explain a cash flow statement, you need to know who to turn to for specific areas of life. This is where effective networking comes into play.

Networking is all about building connections that align with your purpose. Here are several ways to define networking:

1. An interconnected system of people or things.
2. A communication system, like broadcasting stations, that transmits the same programs.
3. An open fabric woven together.
4. A system of intersecting lines or channels, like a railroad or network of canals.
5. In electronics, a system of interconnected components or circuits.
6. To communicate within a group to achieve goals.

This last definition—*to communicate within a group*—requires action. When done correctly, networking leads to tangible outcomes, much like these other examples.

Let's Start Networking!

The Apostle Paul paints a clear picture of how we all play a part in each other's growth. In **1 Corinthians 3:6-7**, he says, *"I planted, Apollos watered, but God gave the growth. So neither the one who plants nor the one who waters is anything, but only God who gives the growth."* We each have a role to play in the lives of those around us, but it's God who ultimately brings everything to fruition.

Networking is more than just building connections; it's about nurturing the relationships that God has placed in your life. It involves acknowledging the people who support you, encourage you, and help you grow. Now, let's explore how you, as the Leading Lady, can start directing your "supporting cast" in a way that benefits both you and them.

How a Leading Lady Does Networking

As the Leading Lady, your Supporting Cast plays a vital role. They bring your role to life and help you thrive. Think about the people who have added the most value to your journey. Who pushed you forward when you wanted to step back? Who encourages you to reach your full potential? And who might God be placing in your life for the future?

Reflect on Your Past: Consider those who have influenced your life thus far. Who helped you in moments of doubt or uncertainty?

- **Scripture**: *"Therefore encourage one another and build up each other, as indeed you are doing."* – **1 Thessalonians 5:11**
- **Application**: Write down the names of those who have

supported you in the past. Reflect on how they shaped your journey and consider reconnecting with them if needed.

Evaluate Your Present: Look at the people around you today. Who is cheering you on in your current season? Are there mentors, friends, or colleagues adding value to your life right now?

- **Scripture**: *"Iron sharpens iron, and one person sharpens the wits of another."* – **Proverbs 27:17**
- **Application**: Create a list of the people in your life who encourage your growth. Pray for them and look for ways to strengthen those relationships.

Prepare for the Future: Ask God to lead you to the right people in the future—those who will help you grow spiritually, emotionally, and professionally. These connections may not be obvious now, but trust that God has a plan to place the right individuals in your life at the right time.

- **Scripture**: *"The steps of a good man are ordered by the Lord..."* – **Psalm 37:23a**
- **Application**: Pray for guidance as you build new relationships. Stay open to new connections and opportunities that God brings your way, trusting that He is directing your path.

Your Supporting Cast: Managing Relationships

Your Supporting Cast doesn't just consist of people from your past or present; it also includes those who will continue to shape your future. These individuals bring value and perspective to your journey, but it's important to understand the dynamics of each relationship:

- **Those Who Empower You**: These are the mentors and friends who build you up, offering experience, wisdom, and insight to help you reach new heights.
- **Those You Empower**: Just as you have received empowerment, you are also called to pour into others. Use your resources, wisdom, and influence to help others become the best versions of themselves. *"Bear one another's burdens, and in this way, you will fulfill the law of Christ."* – **Galatians 6:2**

Building Your Network

Jot Down Key Connections: Make a list of people who have played pivotal roles in your life, as well as those who continue to guide you. Keep their contact information close—whether it's their phone number, address, or email. These connections are part of your Life Script.

- **Scripture**: *"A friend loves at all times, and kinsfolk are born to share adversity."* – **Proverbs 17:17**
- **Application**: Add these key people to your address book and appreciate them for being a part of your life. They will be an invaluable resource as you move forward.

Recognize Your Influence: Understand that just as you've been impacted by others, you too have the power to impact those around you. Use your influence wisely, knowing that your actions can shape lives.

- **Scripture**: *"Let each of you look not to your own interests, but to the interests of others."* – **Philippians 2:4**
- **Application**: Reflect on areas of your life where you have the opportunity to positively influence others. Write down three ways you can use your gifts and influence to help someone else. Pray for wisdom on how to best serve and support the people around you.

The Leading Lady's Next Step: Taking Control of Your Network

Your Supporting Cast plays a vital role in your life's production. From those who empower you to those you empower, the connections you build influence your success as the Leading Lady. Maintaining and nurturing these relationships takes intentionality, but the reward is immeasurable. As you move forward, lean into the relationships God has blessed you with and be open to the new ones He will place in your path.

This is the role of a lifetime—and your Supporting Cast is there with you, cheering you on every step of the way.

Scripture References:

- Philippians 4:13
- Ecclesiastes 3:1-2

- 1 Corinthians 3:6, 7
- 1 Thessalonians 5:11
- Proverbs 27:17
- Psalm 37:23a
- Galatians 6:2
- Proverbs 17:17
- Philippians 2:4

Rehearsing for Success – Practice Makes Perfect

REHEARSAL – *Re-doing what you hear* – **PRACTICE makes PERFECT**

You are now stepping into the role you were always meant to play. God wrote a script specifically designed for you, the Director chose you, and your Agent guides you daily as you advance from understudy to lead. Your audition for this life role was predetermined before birth, and now that you know your cast and have developed the necessary connections, it's time to solidify your performance through constant rehearsal.

Rehearsal is where the real work happens. It's where you develop the habits, mindset, and actions that will keep you on the path to success. **Proverbs 3:5-6** reminds us: *"Trust in the Lord with all your heart, and do not rely on your own insight. In all your ways acknowledge him, and he will make straight your paths."* Rehearsal is about repeating what you hear from God, practicing His principles, and making them a part of your daily life. It's about "redoing" what you hear—taking God's Word and living it out.

The Word of God says: *"... let everyone be quick to listen, slow to speak, slow to anger;..."* – **James 1:19b**. And, *"So faith comes from what is heard, and what is heard comes through the word of Christ."* – **Romans 10:17**. As you practice and perfect your role, remember that every step is important to maintaining your lead. **Psalms 37:23** says: *"The steps of a good man are ordered by the Lord, when He delights in our way."*

Steps of a Leading Lady

Here are the steps that will guide you as you rehearse and perfect your walk as the Leading Lady in your life story:

Self-Control: Self-control is the ability to manage your emotions, desires, and actions, even in challenging situations. It's about responding thoughtfully instead of reacting impulsively, staying disciplined, and making choices that align with God's will. The first step in your journey is self-control.

- **Scripture: 1 Peter 1:13** says: *"Therefore, prepare your minds for action; be self-controlled; set your hope fully on the grace to be given you when Jesus Christ is revealed."*
- **Application**: Practice self-control in everyday situations by taking a moment to pause before reacting. Whether it's controlling anger, resisting temptation, or curbing impulsive decisions, remind yourself that God has equipped you with the ability to stay disciplined and focused.
- **Additional Scripture**: *"But the fruit of the Spirit is love, joy, peace, forbearance, kindness, goodness, faithfulness, gentleness and self-control."* – **Galatians 5:22-23**

Restoration: Restoration is about God's promise to renew and heal the broken areas of your life.

- **Scripture:** God promises in **Joel 2:25a, 26 (NKJV):** *"I will restore to you the years that the swarming locust has eaten... You shall eat in plenty and be satisfied, and praise the name of the Lord your God, Who has dealt wondrously with you; And My people shall never be put to shame."*
- **Application:** Reflect on areas of your life where you need restoration—whether emotional, relational, or spiritual. Trust God to restore what was lost and look for opportunities to renew your faith, relationships, and purpose.
- **Additional Scripture:** *"The Lord is near to the brokenhearted and saves the crushed in spirit."* – **Psalm 34:18**

Surrender: This involves letting go of your own plans and trusting God with every area of your life.

To be restored, you must surrender.

- **Scripture: Matthew 16:24-25** says: *"If any want to become my followers, let them deny themselves and take up their cross and follow me. For those who want to save their life will lose it, and those who lose their life for my sake will find it."*
- **Application:** Surrender the areas of your life that you've been holding onto, whether it's control over situations, fear, or pride. Submit these to God, knowing that He can work wonders when you let go of your own plans and

trust His.

- **Additional Scripture**: *"Humble yourselves, therefore, under God's mighty hand, that he may lift you up in due time."* – **1 Peter 5:6**

Examination: Alongside surrender comes examination. It's the process of taking an honest look at your life, choices, and spiritual walk.

- **Scripture: Lamentations 3:40** says: *"Let us test and examine our ways, and return to the Lord."*
- **Application**: Set aside time regularly to examine your life. Ask yourself whether your actions and choices align with God's will. If you find areas where you've strayed, seek His forgiveness and guidance for moving forward.
- **Additional Scripture**: *"Search me, O God, and know my heart; test me and know my thoughts."* – **Psalm 139:23**

Confession: Once you've examined your life, confession follows.

- **Scripture: James 5:16** encourages us to *"confess your sins to each other and pray for each other so that you may be healed."* Confession brings healing—it acknowledges your mistakes, releasing you from guilt and burden.
- **Application**: Confess your mistakes to God and to trusted people in your life. Be open about your struggles and ask for prayer and accountability. This will bring healing and set you free from shame.
- **Additional Scripture**: *"If we confess our sins, he who is faithful and just will forgive us our sins and cleanse us from*

all unrighteousness." – **1 John 1:9**

Deliverance: Deliverance is the freedom that comes when God removes the chains holding you back. You have been set free from fear, doubt, or past hurts.

- **Scripture: Psalm 34:17** says: *"When the righteous cry for help, the Lord hears, and rescues them from all their troubles."*
- **Application**: Identify the things that have been holding you back—whether it's fear, doubt, or past hurts—and cry out to God for deliverance. Trust that He will remove those barriers and set you free to walk in His purpose.
- **Additional Scripture**: *"For freedom Christ has set us free. Stand firm, therefore, and do not submit again to a yoke of slavery."* – **Galatians 5:1**

Discipline: Discipline is the structure that allows you to stay on track that helps you grow spiritually and maintain the habits that support your role.

- **Scripture: Hebrews 12:11** tells us: *"Now, discipline always seems painful rather than pleasant at the time, but later it yields the peaceful fruit of righteousness to those who have been trained by it."*
- **Application**: Create routines that foster spiritual growth—such as daily prayer, Bible study, or journaling. Discipline will help you maintain the habits that support your role as the Leading Lady.
- **Additional Scripture**: *"for God did not give us a spirit of*

cowardice, but rather a spirit of power and of love and of self-discipline." – **2 Timothy 1:7**

Forgiveness: Forgiveness is about letting go of hurt and resentment to find peace and freedom.

- **Scripture: Ephesians 4:32** encourages us to *"and be kind to one another, tenderhearted, forgiving one another, as God in Christ has forgiven you."*
- **Application:** Reflect on any grudges or hurts that you've been holding onto. Ask God for the strength to forgive others and yourself, allowing you to move forward in freedom.
- **Additional Scripture:** *"For if you forgive other people when they sin against you, your heavenly Father will also forgive you."* – **Matthew 6:14**

Correction: It involves accepting God's guidance to make adjustments in your life.

- **Scripture: Proverbs 3:12 (NKJV)** says: *"For whom the Lord loves He corrects, Just as a father the son in whom he delights."*
- **Application:** Be open to God's correction and direction in your life. When things don't go as planned, seek to learn from the experience and realign yourself with His will.
- **Additional Scripture:** *"Whoever loves discipline loves knowledge, but whoever hates correction is stupid."* – **Proverbs 12:1**

Reflection: Reflection allows you to look back on your journey to learn and grow from your experiences.

- **Scripture: Psalm 119:15** says: *"I will meditate on your precepts and consider your ways."*
- **Application**: Set aside time to reflect on how far you've come, and the lessons God has taught you. Celebrate your progress, and let it fuel your confidence for the future.
- **Additional Scripture**: *"Remember the days of old; consider the generations long past. Ask your father and he will tell you, your elders, and they will explain to you."* – **Deuteronomy 32:7**

Meditation: Meditation is about spending quiet time with God, allowing His Word to settle deeply in your heart.

- **Scripture: Joshua 1:8** instructs us to *"keep this Book of the Law always on your lips; meditate on it day and night."*
- **Application**: Spend time each day meditating on God's Word. Let it fill your heart and guide your actions. This will help you stay grounded and focused on your role.
- **Additional Scripture**: *"But they delight in the law of the Lord, meditating on it day and night."* – **Psalm 1:2**

Enlightenment: Enlightenment is the moment where everything comes together, and you fully understand God's purpose for your life.

- **Scripture: Psalm 119:105** says: *"Your word is a lamp for my feet, a light on my path."*

- **Application**: As you reach this stage, embrace the clarity and wisdom God has given you. Continue walking in His light, using your role as a Leading Lady to inspire and uplift others.
- **Additional Scripture**: *"The unfolding of your words gives light; it gives understanding to the simple."* – **Psalm 119:130**

As you continue rehearsing these principles, you are being prepared for your **Showtime**. This chapter is about perfecting your craft and learning the steps that will lead you to shine in your role as the Leading Lady. But remember, the journey doesn't end here. In fact, it's just beginning. All the preparation, discipline, and growth have led you to this moment—the moment where the curtain rises, and it's time for you to shine.

Scripture References:

- Proverbs 3:5-6
- James 1:19b
- Romans 10:17
- Psalms 37:23
- 1 Peter 1:13
- Galatians 5:22-23
- Joel 2:25a, 26 (NKJV)
- Psalm 34:18
- Matthew 16:24-25
- 1 Peter 5:6
- Lamentations 3:40
- Psalm 139:23

- James 5:16
- 1 John 1:9
- Psalm 34:17
- Galatians 5:1
- Hebrews 12:11
- 2 Timothy 1:7
- Ephesians 4:32
- Matthew 6:14
- Proverbs 3:12 (NKJV)
- Proverbs 12:1
- Psalm 119:15
- Deuteronomy 32:7
- Joshua 1:8
- Psalm 1:2
- Psalm 119:105
- Psalm 119:130

Showtime – Stepping into the Spotlight

What is a Leading Lady's Showtime? It's her time to soar, the moment when all the preparation, rehearsing, and practice ends, and she steps into her destiny. There is no more practicing or hiding in the shadows—it's time for the curtain to roll back, and for her to take her place center stage.

In 1987, a syndicated show was broadcasted that became a household name— **"It's Showtime at the Apollo."** Families stayed up late on Saturday nights just to catch this show. The Apollo Theater, located in Harlem, New York, featured live performances and became the breaking ground for up-and-coming artists. The spotlight at the Apollo was a place where dreams were realized, where stars were born. Similarly, God has His own version of Showtime for His leading ladies—where you step into the role He has prepared for you, fulfilling your destiny and walking into your preordained future. It's the moment when you stop hiding, stop rehearsing, and fully embrace the path God has laid out for you.

Throughout the Bible, we see how God's leading ladies emerged in times where they were often hidden among the culture of men. Yet, when their Showtime arrived, they stepped into the spotlight and brought about significant change, with some even saving nations. For these women, Showtime meant stepping out of obscurity and stepping into their divine calling.

One of these leading ladies was **Rahab**, a woman with a scandalous past who emerged from the shadows to become a light of providence. The book of Joshua tells us about the Israelite spies who were sent to scout the land on the other side of the Jordan River. These spies found shelter in the home of Rahab, a prostitute in Jericho. When the king of Jericho learned about the spies, he sent orders to Rahab to bring them out. However, Rahab hid the men on her roof and sent the king's men on a wild goose chase. This was the beginning of her conversion—a moment where she moved out of the shadows of her former life.

Rahab acknowledged the power of the God of Israel, and her testimony for her people was profound:

"For we have heard of the Lord's feats, how He dried up the water of the Red Sea for you when you came out of Egypt, and what you did to Sihon and Og, the two kings of the Amorites east of the Jordan, whom you completely destroyed. When we heard of it, our hearts melted in fear and everyone's courage failed because of you, for the Lord your God is God in heaven above and on the earth below." – **Joshua 2:10-11**

Rahab's transformation from a prostitute to a hero of faith was her moment to step into the spotlight. She seized her Showtime, and through her faith, not only was her family saved, but she secured her place in the lineage of Jesus Christ (***Matthew 1:5***).

Just like **"Showtime at the Apollo"** gave aspiring artists their moment to shine, God offers each of us our own Showtime—the moment when our faith, preparation, and resilience come together, and we step into the fullness of our calling.

What Does Showtime Look Like for You?

Your Showtime is the pivotal moment when everything you've practiced, rehearsed, and prayed for finally aligns. It's the moment when you take center stage in your life and fully embrace the role God has prepared for you. Like Rahab, your Showtime may arrive in unexpected ways and at a time when others might not expect you to shine. But when God says it's time, no one can stand in your way.

Recognizing your moments of opportunity is key to stepping into your personal "Showtime." These are the moments where your faith and readiness converge. Here's how to recognize and embrace your Showtime:

Reflect on your preparation: Look back at the lessons God has been teaching you. Every challenge, trial, or success has been part of your rehearsal.

- **Scripture:** *"My brothers and sisters, whenever you face trials of any kind, consider it nothing but joy, because you know that the testing of your faith produces endurance; "* – **James 1:2, 3**
- **Application**: Write down key lessons you've learned through the ups and downs of life. These will serve as reminders of how God has equipped you for this moment.

Be aware of divine timing: Sometimes, our moments to shine come when we least expect them. Trust that God's timing is perfect.

- **Scripture:** *"He has made everything suitable for its time;."*

– **Ecclesiastes 3:11**
- **Application**: Pray for discernment to recognize when God is calling you into a new season or opportunity.

Embracing the Spotlight

Stepping into the spotlight can be intimidating. The spotlight exposes everything—your strengths and your vulnerabilities. But remember, this is your moment, and God has equipped you for it. Just like an actress who rehearses her lines, perfects her craft, and waits for her cue, you have been preparing for this moment. There's no more hiding, no more understudy roles—this is your time to shine.

You may wonder if you're ready, but know that God has already deemed you ready. You've done the work, gone through the trials, and now it's time to walk boldly into your Showtime. Just as Rahab left her past behind and embraced her divine opportunity, you too must let go of what no longer serves you and trust in God's plan.

Overcoming fear and doubt is essential when stepping into your moment. Remember that God has already equipped you to succeed:

Acknowledge your readiness: God doesn't call the equipped; He equips the called. Trust in His preparation and your growth.

- **Scripture**: *"For we are what he has made us, created in Christ Jesus for good works, which God prepared beforehand to be our way of life."* – **Ephesians 2:10**
- **Application**: Write a declaration that affirms, "I am ready

for my Showtime because God has prepared me through [insert a personal challenge]." Place it somewhere visible.

Let go of the past: Just as Rahab left her past behind, you must leave behind the things that no longer serve you.

- **Scripture**: *"Do not remember the former things or consider the things of old. I am doing a new thing!"* – **Isaiah 43:18, 19a**
- **Application**: Identify past experiences, relationships, or habits that have held you back. Take a symbolic action like writing them down and discarding or burning the list.

The Impact of Your Performance

When you step into your Showtime, it's not just about you—it's about the lives that will be touched and inspired by your story. Your story, your transformation, and your growth have the power to inspire others. Just like audiences watched in awe at the Apollo Theater as stars were born, people will watch how you handle your moment in the spotlight. Will you embrace it with confidence, knowing God is guiding your steps, or will you shy away?

Consider other leading ladies from the Bible who stepped boldly into their Showtime:

- **Esther**, who risked her life to save her people, declared, *"If I perish, I perish"* – **Esther 4:16**. Her moment in the spotlight saved a nation.

- **Deborah**, a judge and prophetess, stepped into leadership in a time when women were not expected to lead. Her courage brought victory to Israel.
- **Mary**, the mother of Jesus, answered the call with humility and grace, saying, *"Here am I, the servant of the Lord; let it be with me according to your word"* – **Luke 1:38**. She embraced her destiny, changing the course of history.

These women remind us that stepping into our Showtime is not just about personal success—it's about fulfilling a greater purpose. Your life, like theirs, can have a ripple effect that impacts generations to come.

As you step into your moment, remember the broader impact of your actions:

Consider your influence: Who is watching you, and how can your journey inspire them? Your choices and actions may become the testimony that encourages someone else.

- **Scripture:** *"In the same way, let your light shine before others, that they may see your good deeds and glorify your Father in heaven."* – **Matthew 5:16**
- **Application:** Identify three people who are watching your journey. Pray for them and ask God to use your story to inspire and strengthen their faith.

Preparing for Your Moment

As you prepare to step into your Showtime, take a moment to reflect on the journey that led you here. You've rehearsed through the trials and triumphs. You've learned the lessons of faith, self-control, and surrender. You've built resilience through forgiveness, correction, and discipline. Now, you're ready to apply everything you've learned.

Here are a few final reminders as you step into the spotlight:

Trust in your preparation: God has been with you through every rehearsal. You are ready for this moment.

- **Scripture**: *"Trust in the Lord with all your heart, and do not rely on your own insight. In all your ways acknowledge him, and he will make straight your paths"* – **Proverbs 3:5-6**.

Know your worth: Just like Rahab, Esther, and Deborah, you are valuable and equipped for the role God has given you.

- **Scripture**: *"But you are a chosen race, a royal priesthood, a holy nation, God's own people, in order that you may proclaim the mighty acts of him who called you out of darkness into his marvelous light"* – **1 Peter 2:9**.

Be bold: Do not fear the spotlight. God has called you to it for a reason, and He will guide your every step.

- **Scripture**: *"I can do all things through him who strengthens me"* – **Philippians 4:13**.

Remember your audience: Your Showtime is not just for you—it's for everyone who can be touched and inspired by your story.

- **Scripture**: *"In the same way, let your light shine before others, so that they may see your good works and give glory to your Father in heaven"* – **Matthew 5:16**.

Your Cue to Step into the Spotlight

The stage is set, the audience is waiting, and now the spotlight is on you. As the curtain rises, know that you are not standing alone. God is with you, guiding your steps, and you are fully prepared to give the performance of your life. The world needs to see the light within you, so don't be afraid to shine brightly.

As you step into your Showtime, remember this is your moment to soar. There's no more rehearsing, no more practicing—this is the real deal. Embrace the role God has prepared for you and step boldly into your destiny. The curtain has risen, and now it's time for you to take center stage.

Scripture References:

- Joshua 2:10-11
- Matthew 1:5
- James 1:2-3
- Ecclesiastes 3:11
- Ephesians 2:10
- Isaiah 43:18-19
- Esther 4:16
- Luke 1:38

- Proverbs 3:5-6
- 1 Peter 2:9
- Philippians 4:13
- Matthew 5:16

Behind the Scenes – Building Inner Strength

Every great performance depends on what happens behind the scenes. While the audience only sees the final act, the true strength of any Leading Lady comes from the preparation, discipline, and resilience she builds when no one is watching. In life, your Showtime will be sustained by the inner work you do in the quiet moments—those critical practices that fortify your spirit, mind, and emotions.

Much like a stage production requires a backstage crew to keep things running smoothly, your inner strength ensures you can shine under life's spotlight. This chapter will focus on cultivating that behind-the-scenes strength so that when your moment comes, you'll stand tall and deliver with grace, power, and confidence.

Spiritual Strength: Staying Connected to Your Source

Your spiritual life is the foundation of your inner strength. Much like a performer relies on their training and skills, you must rely on your connection to God to guide you through life's challenges. Without a strong spiritual foundation, it's easy to become overwhelmed by the pressures and distractions that come with stepping into the spotlight. For every woman, whether juggling a career, family, or personal challenges, this spiritual connection is what sustains you.

Psalm 46:1 reminds us: *"God is our refuge and strength, a very present help in trouble."* Your relationship with God is your greatest source of strength, and staying connected through prayer, meditation, and reflection ensures you have the spiritual resilience to face any challenge.

How to Strengthen Your Spiritual Life:

Daily Prayer

Set aside time each day to connect with God. Whether you're managing a busy household or climbing the corporate ladder, make prayer your daily anchor. It can be a simple conversation with God that helps you regain peace and focus.

- **Scripture**: *"Pray without ceasing."* – **1 Thessalonians 5:17**
- **Application**: Start with short, consistent prayers. You can pray while driving to work, cooking, or even during a break. It's not about how long you pray, but how consistently you stay connected.

Meditation on Scripture

Reflecting on God's Word centers your thoughts and brings you back to His promises, especially during moments of doubt or stress.

- **Scripture**: *"But their delight is in the law of the Lord, and on his law they meditate day and night."* – **Psalm 1:2**
- **Application**: Pick one scripture to meditate on daily. Write it on a card and carry it with you. When faced with stress or confusion, pause to reflect on that verse.

Gratitude Practice

Regularly expressing gratitude keeps your heart open and focused on your blessings. This is especially important in a world that constantly pushes us to want more.

- **Scripture**: *"Give thanks in all circumstances; for this is the will of God in Christ Jesus for you."* – **1 Thessalonians 5:18**
- **Application**: At the end of each day, write down three things you're grateful for. Whether it's a small victory or simply a moment of peace, gratitude strengthens your connection to God and shifts your focus from what's lacking to what's present.

Mental Strength: Building Resilience and Focus

Mental strength is your ability to stay focused and maintain a positive mindset, even when things get tough. In the same way an actress must remain composed under pressure, you must learn to control your thoughts and stay disciplined. For many women, mental resilience is key to balancing life's many demands—from managing work, home, and personal development.

Proverbs 23:7 (NKJV) tells us: *"For as he think in his hearts, so is he."* What you believe and dwell on will shape your reality. By cultivating mental resilience, you can face obstacles with confidence and avoid being derailed by fear or doubt.

How to Build Mental Resilience:

Positive Affirmations

Repeating affirmations can rewire your mind to focus on the positive and reinforce your confidence. For example, *"I am capable, I am strong, I am prepared for my moment."*

- **Scripture**: *"I can do all things through him who strengthens me."* – **Philippians 4:13**
- **Application**: Begin each day with positive affirmations. Speak these affirmations over yourself in the morning to prepare your mind for the challenges ahead. It could be as simple as saying, *"Today, I will embrace challenges with grace."*

Focus on Solutions, Not Problems

Train your mind to look for solutions instead of getting stuck in worry or anxiety. Every challenge is an opportunity for growth.

- **Scripture**: *"We know that all things work together for good for those who love God, who are called according to his purpose."* – **Romans 8:28**
- **Application**: When facing a challenge, ask yourself, *"What is one step I can take to move forward?"* Focus on action rather than dwelling on the issue itself.

Practice Mindfulness

Staying present in the moment, rather than being consumed by what happened in the past or worrying about the future, helps you maintain focus and clarity.

- **Scripture**: *"So do not worry about tomorrow, for tomorrow will bring worries of its own. Today's trouble is enough for today."* – **Matthew 6:34**
- **Application**: Throughout your day, pause and take three deep breaths to center yourself. Whether you're dealing with stress at work or at home, this simple practice will bring you back to the present moment.

Emotional Strength: Cultivating Balance and Self-Awareness

Emotional strength means maintaining balance and self-awareness, even when emotions run high. Just as an actress must master her emotions to deliver a powerful performance, you need to manage your feelings and stay grounded. For women navigating the complexities of relationships, career transitions, or personal growth, emotional resilience is vital.

Philippians 4:6-7 advises: *"Do not worry about anything, but in everything by prayer and supplication with thanksgiving let your requests be made known to God. And the peace of God, which surpasses all understanding, will guard your hearts and your minds in Christ Jesus."* When you trust in God's plan, you can handle emotional challenges with grace.

How to Cultivate Emotional Strength:

Journaling

Writing down your thoughts and feelings helps you process emotions and gain clarity. Journaling can also reveal patterns in your emotional responses, helping you identify areas for growth.

- **Scripture**: *"Let the words of my mouth and the meditation of my heart be acceptable to you, O Lord, my rock and my redeemer."* – **Psalm 19:14**
- **Application**: Spend 10 minutes at the end of each day journaling about how you felt. Did you feel frustrated, happy, or overwhelmed? This practice helps you reflect on the source of your emotions and how you can respond differently.

Set Healthy Boundaries

Protecting your emotional energy means knowing when to say no. It's essential to set boundaries with people or situations that drain you.

- **Scripture**: *"Keep your heart with all vigilance, for from it flow the springs of life."* – **Proverbs 4:23**
- **Application**: Identify one area of your life where you need to set better boundaries. This could mean saying no to extra responsibilities or creating more time for self-care. Communicate these boundaries with kindness and clarity.

Practice Self-Compassion

Be kind to yourself when things don't go as planned. Setbacks are part of growth, and it's important to give yourself grace during difficult moments.

- **Scripture**: *"The Lord is merciful and gracious, slow to anger and abounding in steadfast love."* – **Psalm 103:8**

- **Application**: When you make a mistake or fall short, remind yourself that it's okay not to have everything together. Offer yourself the same kindness you'd offer a friend.

Scripture References:

- Psalm 46:1
- 1 Thessalonians 5:17
- Psalm 1:2
- 1 Thessalonians 5:18
- Proverbs 23:7 (NKJV)
- Philippians 4:13
- Romans 8:28
- Matthew 6:34
- Philippians 4:6-7
- Psalm 19:14
- Proverbs 4:23
- Psalm 103:8

Handling Criticism – Navigating the Reviews

As the Leading Lady in your own life, stepping into the spotlight means you're bound to receive feedback. Some will be uplifting and helpful, but not all of it. Handling criticism is an essential skill, both for personal growth and to maintain your confidence when the pressure is on.

Just like performers face reviews from critics, you will experience opinions from people around you—and even from your own inner critic. These "reviews" may sometimes feel harsh, but learning to discern the value in feedback, respond with grace, and filter out negativity is a vital part of your journey.

The Role of Feedback in Growth

Feedback, whether positive or negative, is part of life's learning process. For women at any stage of life, learning to receive correction with humility is key to growth. **Proverbs 12:1** tells us: *"Whoever loves discipline loves knowledge, but whoever hates correction is stupid."* This scripture emphasizes the importance of receiving correction as a tool for growth.

Whether it's feedback in your career, personal life, or even on how you manage your time, every note offers an opportunity to improve. God uses feedback to mold us into the version of ourselves that He has envisioned.

How to Embrace Constructive Criticism:

Discern the Source

Not every voice is worth listening to. Consider the person offering feedback—are they someone whose opinion you value?

- **Scripture**: *"The ear that listens to life-giving reproof will dwell among the wise."* – **Proverbs 15:31 (ESV)**
- **Application**: Before accepting criticism, take a moment to ask, "Is this person speaking from a place of care and understanding, or are they projecting their own limitations on me?"

Separate Emotion from Truth

Criticism can sting, but you must separate the emotional response from the constructive elements.

- **Scripture**: *"A fool gives full vent to anger, but the wise quietly holds it back."* – **Proverbs 29:11**
- **Application**: Before reacting, step away and calm your emotions. Reflect on what can be learned. This will help you approach feedback with a clear mind.

Ask for Clarification

If feedback feels unclear or unfair, don't be afraid to ask for more details.

- **Scripture**: *"The purposes in the human mind are like deep water, but the intelligent will draw them out."* – **Proverbs**

20:5

- **Application**: A simple, "Can you give me an example of what you mean?" can lead to better understanding and allow you to take action.

Responding with Grace

How you respond to criticism affects both your personal growth and your relationships. Responding with grace shows strength of character, regardless of how the feedback is delivered. Even when the criticism feels hurtful, your gracious response demonstrates that you are willing to learn and grow.

Steps to Respond Gracefully:

Pause Before Reacting

When receiving criticism, take a moment to process before responding.

- **Scripture**: *"You must understand this, my beloved: let everyone be quick to listen, slow to speak, slow to anger." –* **James 1:19**
- **Application**: Before replying, take a deep breath, pray for discernment, and consider the content rather than reacting emotionally.

Thank the Critic

Even when the feedback stings, thanking the person offering it shows maturity and openness.

- **Scripture**: *"Do not repay anyone evil for evil, but take thought for what is noble in the sight of all."* – **Romans 12:17**
- **Application**: Simply say, "Thank you for sharing," even if you disagree. This shows you are willing to listen, and it opens the door for respectful communication.

Use Feedback for Growth

After evaluating the criticism, use what is helpful to improve.

- **Scripture**: *"Give instruction to the wise, and they will become wiser still; teach the righteous and they will gain in learning."* – **Proverbs 9:9**
- **Application**: Keep a "growth journal" where you write down constructive feedback. Reflect on how it has helped you grow and celebrate those moments of improvement.

Filtering Out Negativity

Not all criticism is valuable or constructive. There will be times when feedback is rooted in jealousy, bitterness, or misunderstanding. Learning to filter out negative, non-constructive criticism is important for protecting your peace and confidence.

How to Handle Unfair or Negative Criticism:

Consider the Source's Intentions

Is the criticism meant to build you up, or is it coming from a place of insecurity or malice?

- **Scripture**: *"A perverse person stirs up conflict, and a gossip separates close friends."* – **Proverbs 16:28 (NIV)**
- **Application**: Recognize when someone's criticism is based on their own issues. Their negativity doesn't define your worth.

Don't Internalize Negativity

If the criticism is unfair, remember that your worth comes from God.

- **Scripture**: *"Keep your heart with all vigilance, for from it flow the springs of life."* – **Proverbs 4:23**
- **Application**: When faced with hurtful feedback, remind yourself that your value is not determined by others but by God's view of you.

Keep Your Confidence

Don't let negative feedback shake your confidence.

- **Scripture**: *"For the Lord will be your confidence and will keep your foot from being caught."* – **Proverbs 3:26**
- **Application**: In moments of self-doubt, turn to scripture and prayer to reinforce your confidence in God's plan for you.

Dealing with Your Inner Critic

Sometimes the harshest feedback comes from within. Your inner critic can be louder than any external voice, constantly pointing out your flaws or doubts. To silence this voice, you must remind yourself of who you are in God's eyes.

How to Silence Your Inner Critic:

Speak Truth Over Lies

Combat negative self-talk with God's truth.

- **Scripture**: *"I praise you, for I am fearfully and wonderfully made..."* – **Psalm 139:14a**
- **Application**: Create a list of affirmations based on scripture. When your inner critic speaks, counter it with God's promises for your life.

Focus on Progress, Not Perfection

Your journey is about growth, not perfection.

- **Scripture**: *"I am confident of this, that the one who began a good work among you will bring it to completion..."* – **Philippians 1:6a**
- **Application**: Keep track of how far you've come, rather than focusing on where you've fallen short. Progress is a process, not a destination.

Practice Self-Compassion

Be kind to yourself when things don't go as planned.

- **Scripture**: *"The Lord is gracious and merciful, slow to anger and abounding in steadfast love."* – **Psalm 145:8**
- **Application**: When you stumble, remember that God's grace is more than enough to cover your imperfections.

Celebrating Positive Feedback and Self-Acceptance

Embracing positive feedback is just as important as handling criticism. Learn to celebrate compliments and self-acceptance as part of your growth journey.

How to Celebrate and Accept Praise:

Receive Compliments Graciously

Learn to accept praise with humility and gratitude.

- **Scripture**: *"Let another praise you, and not your own mouth— a stranger, and not your own lips."* – **Proverbs 27:2**
- **Application**: The next time someone offers a compliment, say "thank you" instead of brushing it off. This reflects your growth and confidence.

Acknowledge Your Progress

Reflect on how far you've come and celebrate your milestones.

- **Scripture**: *"But let each one examine his own work, and then he will have rejoicing in himself alone, and not in another."* – **Galatians 6:4 (NKJV)**
- **Application**: At the end of each week, reflect on your

progress and thank God for the strength and wisdom that brought you this far.

Give Glory to God

Always remember to give credit to God for your gifts and achievements.

- **Scripture**: "...*whatever you do, do everything for the glory of God.*" – **1 Corinthians 10:31(b)**
- **Application**: After any achievement or recognition, take a moment to thank God for guiding and empowering you.

Scripture References:

- Proverbs 12:1
- Proverbs 15:31 (ESV)
- Proverbs 29:11
- Proverbs 20:5
- James 1:19
- Romans 12:17
- Proverbs 9:9
- Proverbs 16:28 (NIV)
- Proverbs 4:23
- Proverbs 3:26
- Psalm 139:14a
- Philippians 1:6a
- Psalm 145:8
- Proverbs 27:2

- Galatians 6:4 (NKJV)
- 1 Corinthians 10:31(b)

Encore! Maintaining Your Star Status

Stepping into the spotlight is a remarkable achievement, but the true test of success lies in your ability to sustain it. Just as a star performer may receive an encore after a breathtaking performance, your Showtime doesn't end after one moment of success. The real challenge is how you continue to grow, evolve, and maintain your star status in the face of new challenges and responsibilities.

Your Encore is about consistency, perseverance, and remaining humble amidst success. It's about continuing to live out your purpose even after reaching a milestone. Whether in your personal life, career, or spiritual journey, maintaining your star status requires an ongoing commitment to self-improvement and an open heart to serve others.

Continual Growth: Never Stop Learning

Success can sometimes make us complacent. Once you've reached a certain level of achievement, it's tempting to rest on your laurels. However, true success requires a mindset of continual learning and growth. Like a performer who continually refines their craft, you too must keep evolving. Growth isn't a one-time event; it's a lifelong journey.

Proverbs 9:9 reminds us, *"Give instruction to the wise, and they will become wiser still; teach the righteous and they will gain in learning."* This scripture highlights the importance of remaining teachable, even after achieving success. No matter how far you've come, there is always more to learn.

Ways to Continue Growing:

Seek New Challenges

Don't settle into comfort. Look for opportunities that stretch you beyond your current capabilities.

- **Scripture**: *"Beloved, I do not consider that I have made it my own; but this one thing I do: forgetting what lies behind and straining forward to what lies ahead, I press on toward the goal for the prize of the heavenly call of God in Christ Jesus."* – **Philippians 3:13, 14**
- **Application**: Regularly assess areas in your life where you can challenge yourself. What's the next step to take? Set goals that push you beyond your comfort zone and develop new skills.

Remain Open to Feedback

Even after success, feedback remains valuable.

- **Scripture**: *"Listen to advice and accept instruction, that you may gain wisdom for the future."* – **Proverbs 19:20**
- **Application**: Seek honest feedback from people who challenge you to grow. Regularly reflect on how constructive criticism can refine your abilities and keep

you grounded.

Expand Your Knowledge

Growth comes from curiosity and openness to new experiences.

- **Scripture**: *"An intelligent mind acquires knowledge, and the ear of the wise seeks knowledge."* – **Proverbs 18:15**
- **Application**: Stay committed to learning through books, seminars, or conversations with others. Seek opportunities to expand your knowledge and grow spiritually and mentally.

Humility: Staying Grounded Amid Success

As you experience success, it's easy to focus on your own achievements and lose sight of the bigger picture. Humility is the key to maintaining your star status without losing your grounding. It's about recognizing that your talents and successes are gifts from God, and that your role as a Leading Lady is not just about you—it's about using your platform to serve others.

Micah 6:8 reminds us, *"He has told you, O mortal, what is good; and what does the Lord require of you but to do justice, and to love kindness, and to walk humbly with your God?"* This scripture calls us to walk humbly, even in success. Humility magnifies accomplishments by keeping your heart aligned with God's purpose.

How to Stay Humble in Success:

Give Credit to God

Always remember that it is God who has given you the strength and talents to succeed.

- **Scripture**: *"So, whether you eat or drink, or whatever you do, do everything for the glory of God."* – **1 Corinthians 10:31**
- **Application**: Make it a habit to thank God in moments of success. Reflect on how you can use your achievements to glorify Him and serve others.

Serve Others

Stay grounded by focusing on service. When you use your gifts to lift others, success becomes about impacting the world, not just personal achievements.

- **Scripture**: *"Like good stewards of the manifold grace of God, serve one another with whatever gift each of you has received."* – **1 Peter 4:10**
- **Application**: Find ways to give back through mentoring or volunteering. Use your platform to help others grow and succeed.

Practice Gratitude

Gratitude is key to staying humble.

- **Scripture**: *"O give thanks to the Lord, for he is good; for his steadfast love endures forever."* – **Psalm 107:1**
- **Application**: Keep a gratitude journal. Regularly write

down things you're thankful for to keep your heart centered on God's goodness.

Perseverance: The Key to Longevity

Success isn't about just reaching a milestone—it's about sustaining it over time. Just as a star performer maintains their craft to stay relevant, you too must persevere through challenges that follow success. Success brings new responsibilities, and perseverance allows you to handle them with grace and resilience.

James 1:12 says, *"Blessed is anyone who endures temptation. Such a one has stood the test and will receive the crown of life that the Lord has promised to those who love him."* Perseverance is about pushing through difficulties and remaining steadfast in your purpose, even when the road becomes hard.

How to Cultivate Perseverance:

Stay Committed to Your Purpose

Don't lose sight of your purpose after achieving success.

- **Scripture**: *"So let us not grow weary in doing what is right, for we will reap at harvest time, if we do not give up."* – **Galatians 6:9**
- **Application**: When challenges arise, remind yourself of your original mission. Stay focused on your calling, and trust that perseverance will lead to greater growth.

Embrace Setbacks as Learning Opportunities

Setbacks are inevitable but can be powerful learning tools.

- **Scripture**: *"My brothers and sisters, whenever you face trials of any kind, consider it nothing but joy, because you know that the testing of your faith produces endurance."* – **James 1:2-3**
- **Application**: When faced with difficulties, reflect on what you can learn. Use setbacks as opportunities to grow, adapt, and refine your approach.

Keep Your Faith at the Center

Perseverance is fueled by faith. When your faith is strong, you can overcome the trials that come with maintaining success.

- **Scripture**: *"I can do all things through him who strengthens me."* – **Philippians 4:13**
- **Application**: Turn to prayer and scripture when doubt or difficulty arises. Let your faith guide you through both the highs and lows.

Closing: The Encore Continues

Just as a performer returns for an encore, your journey doesn't end after Showtime. Your encore is about maintaining your star status with humility, continual growth, and perseverance. Success is not the final destination—it's a steppingstone toward even greater things.

As you continue walking in your purpose, remember that the spotlight is not just for a moment, but for a lifetime of impact. Keep growing, stay humble, and persevere through every challenge, knowing that God is with you every step of the way. Your encore has just begun.

Scripture References:

- Proverbs 9:9
- Philippians 3:13,14
- Proverbs 19:20
- Proverbs 18:15
- Micah 6:8
- 1 Corinthians 10:31
- 1 Peter 4:10
- Psalm 107:1
- James 1:12
- Galatians 6:9
- James 1:2-3
- Philippians 4:13

The Curtain Call – Stepping Fully into Your Role

You've rehearsed, faced the critics, and delivered a stellar performance. Now, as the curtain falls on this act, it's time to reflect on what it means to step fully into your role as the Leading Lady of your life. This isn't the end—it's just the beginning.

For much of your journey, you may have felt like an understudy—waiting in the wings, unsure if your moment would ever come. But God has known the script for your life all along. He's been preparing you for this leading role since the very beginning. As **Jeremiah 1:5** reminds us, *"Before I formed you in the womb I knew you, and before you were born I consecrated you..."* Your path was written by God, and now the spotlight is on you.

This chapter is about fully embracing that role and the responsibilities, opportunities, and challenges that come with it. The Curtain Call isn't just the end of one act—it's the beginning of a life lived with purpose, confidence, and grace as you step into your destiny.

Leaving the Understudy Behind: Embracing Your Purpose

You've spent time preparing behind the scenes, learning your lines, waiting for your moment to step into the spotlight. Now, as the Leading Lady of your story, you must leave behind doubt and hesitation and fully embrace the role you've been destined for.

Many of us feel like we're waiting for permission to be great—unsure if we're ready. But God, the Author of your life, has already qualified you for this moment. **Romans 8:30** reminds us, *"And those whom he predestined he also called; and those whom he called he also justified; and those whom he justified he also glorified."* God has written your role, and now it's time to step confidently into it.

How to Embrace Your Role Fully:

Trust in God's Timing: Transitioning from understudy to Leading Lady is all part of God's perfect plan. Every challenge, every moment of waiting has been preparing you for this role.

- **Scripture**: *"For everything there is a season, and a time for every matter under heaven."* – **Ecclesiastes 3:1**
- **Application**: Reflect on your journey and the lessons God taught you during times of waiting. Trust that your moment is now, and it is all part of His divine timing.

Release Doubt and Fear: As an understudy, doubt may have crept in, but stepping into the lead means trusting that God has equipped you for this moment.

- **Scripture**: *"...Do not fear, for I have redeemed you; I have called you by name, you are mine."* – **Isaiah 43:1(b)**
- **Application**: When doubt arises, remind yourself of God's promises. Speak His truth over your fears, affirming that you are not defined by your past but by God's calling on your life.

Walk in Authority: Now that you've stepped into the lead role, walk with the authority that comes with it. Own your identity, talents, and responsibilities with confidence.

- **Scripture**: *"For God did not give us a spirit of cowardice, but rather a spirit of power and of love and of self-discipline."* – **2 Timothy 1:7**
- **Application**: Stand tall in the role God has written for you, trusting in His power to work through you. Speak life over your circumstances, knowing you walk in His authority.

Stepping into the Fullness of Your Role: Walking in Purpose

Now that you've embraced your role, it's time to live it out fully. Walking in purpose means living each day with intention, knowing that your life has meaning beyond the surface. You're not just filling a role—you're fulfilling a destiny.

Ephesians 2:10 tells us, *"For we are what he has made us, created in Christ Jesus for good works, which God prepared beforehand to be our way of life."* Your purpose has always been part of God's plan. Every gift, talent, and experience you have is part of the good work He's prepared for you.

Living Out Your Role with Purpose:

Align Your Actions with Your Purpose: Every decision you make should align with God's purpose for your life.

- **Scripture**: *"Commit your work to the Lord, and your plans*

will be established." – **Proverbs 16:3**
- **Application**: Evaluate your daily habits and routines. Are they aligned with the purpose God has for you? Make small adjustments to reflect your calling.

Use Your Platform for Good: As the Leading Lady, you have influence in your family, workplace, or community. Use that platform to uplift others and glorify God.

- **Scripture**: *"...Let your light shine before others, so that they may see your good works and give glory to your Father in heaven."* – **Matthew 5:16**
- **Application**: Identify ways you can serve others through your role. Mentor someone, support a cause, or use your influence to make a positive impact.

Keep Growing in Your Role: Stepping into the lead role is just the beginning of a new chapter of growth.

- **Scripture**: *"The path of the righteous is like the light of dawn, which shines brighter and brighter until full day."* – **Proverbs 4:18**
- **Application**: Commit to lifelong growth through study, reflection, and prayer. Make time for activities that foster spiritual and personal development.

The Curtain Call: Reflecting on Your Journey

The Curtain Call is traditionally when the audience acknowledges the performer's work. It's a moment of reflection—both for the audience and the performer—on the journey they've shared. In your life, the Curtain Call is a time to reflect on where you've been, acknowledge the growth you've experienced, and honor God's work in your life.

Philippians 1:6 reminds us, *"I am confident of this, that the one who began a good work among you will bring it to completion by the day of Jesus Christ."* Your journey isn't over, but you've come a long way. Now is the time to reflect on God's faithfulness, your perseverance, and the transformation you've undergone.

How to Reflect on Your Journey:

Celebrate Your Progress: You've stepped into your role and made an impact. Take time to celebrate how far you've come.

- **Scripture**: *"Rejoice in the Lord always; again I will say, Rejoice."* – **Philippians 4:4**
- **Application**: Write down key moments of growth and lessons learned. Celebrate your transformation and the work God has done in your life.

Honor the Journey, Not Just the Destination: While it's important to celebrate where you are, honor the journey that got you here. Every struggle and challenge was part of your process.

- **Scripture**: *"I consider that the sufferings of this present time are not worth comparing with the glory about to be revealed to us."* – **Romans 8:18**

- **Application**: Reflect on past challenges and how God carried you through. Honor both the highs and lows, recognizing their value in shaping your story.

Prepare for the Next Act: The Curtain Call is not the end—it's the beginning of the next phase of your journey. God's plans for you are still unfolding.

- **Scripture**: *"For surely I know the plans I have for you, says the Lord, plans for your welfare and not for harm, to give you a future with hope."* – **Jeremiah 29:11**
- **Application**: Seek God's direction for the next phase. Trust that His plans for you are good, and that the next act will be even more fulfilling than the last.

Closing: Stepping into Eternity's Stage

Your Curtain Call is more than just a moment to reflect—it's an invitation to step into the next chapter with confidence. You've embraced your role as the Leading Lady, and now the world is your stage. But remember, this is only the beginning of a greater journey.

As you move forward, know that God has been with you every step of the way—preparing you, guiding you, and equipping you for this moment. Your role continues to evolve, and there is still much to be written in the story of your life. Keep trusting, keep growing, and keep shining. The curtain may fall on this act, but the next one is already waiting in the wings. Step boldly, for the stage is set, and your light is meant to shine.

Scripture References:

- Jeremiah 1:5
- Romans 8:30
- Ecclesiastes 3:1
- Isaiah 43:1(b)
- 2 Timothy 1:7
- Ephesians 2:10
- Proverbs 16:3
- Matthew 5:16
- Proverbs 4:18
- Philippians 1:6
- Philippians 4:4
- Romans 8:18
- Jeremiah 29:11

Don't miss out!

Visit the website below and you can sign up to receive emails whenever J. L. Foreman publishes a new book. There's no charge and no obligation.

https://books2read.com/r/B-A-CDMMC-IVTAF

BOOKS 2 READ

Connecting independent readers to independent writers.

About the Author

J. L. Foreman is a new author whose writing journey was sparked by a personal spiritual exploration. Born in New Jersey and raised in the small town of Seaford, Delaware, J. L. Foreman grew up in a Christian home that instilled strong values and a deep-rooted faith. This background plays a significant role in her writing, which often delves into themes of faith and life's pivotal moments.

Though she has many hobbies, becoming an author was something that happened unexpectedly, evolving as she pursued other passions. As a proud mother of three beautiful daughters and a handsome son, J. L. Foreman brings a nurturing perspective to her storytelling.

Her debut book is a representation of her spiritual journey, capturing the pinnacle moments of life through the lens of faith. While this work is faith-based, she plans to explore other genres in future projects. J. L. Foreman finds joy in the development of each story, letting her faith and creativity guide her pen.